Questions We All Have Regarding Relationships

By Kyle Smith

EJF Publishing & Printing
Hillside, IL 60162

Copyright© 2010 by Kyle Smith

All rights reserved. Reproduction of text by any means without the express written consent of the author is not permitted. Although the author and publishers have made every effort to ensure the accuracy and completeness of the information contained in this book, we assume no responsibility for errors, inaccuracies, omissions, or any inconsistency therein.

Any slights of people, places, belief systems or organizations are unintentional. Any resemblance to anyone living deceased or somewhere in between is truly coincidental.

For additional copies contact: contact@ejfpublish.com

Printed in the United States of America by:
EJF Publishing and Printing
2205 S Wolf Rd. Suite 151
Hillside, Illinois 60162
http://www.ejfpublish.com/

ISBN-13 978-0-9841797-2-5

Cover Design Concept EJF Publishing & Printing
Cover Photo by: PJ Studio Photography
Interior Editing/Layout: Shadrina Fleming of Fleming Admin Works

Unless otherwise indicated, all scriptural quotations are taken from the King James Version of the Bible or the New International King James Version.

DEDICATION

This book is dedicated to my dearly beloved sister, Fertamia Smith, whom I will love and cherish in my heart forever. I also dedicate it to her four children: Brianna, Jamaal, Joshua, and Charles Jacob, who are near and dear to my heart. There is nothing that I would not go out of my way to do for them.

FOREWORD

While man has figured out how to land on the moon, the subject of love has continued to be a question of debate and one of the most perplexing struggles of the human experience. This inspiring book, authored by Kyle Smith, after the tragic murder of his sister, Fertamia, by an abusive ex-boyfriend, is the go-to manual regarding matters of the heart in contemporary dating "Questions We All Have Regarding Relationships" addresses the most common relationship faux pas and includes real life solutions. This uplifting resource was birthed as a result of an ongoing question and answer forum on a popular social networking site. It has emerged as an accurate, yet uncomplicated compilation of relationship advice. You do not have to read "Questions We All Have Regarding Relationships" in any particular order. Just pick and choose your relationship concerns of the moment as your guide in browsing the book. Ultimately, Kyle desires to leave you lifted, inspired, and savvy in your knowledge of relationships on a romantic and spiritual level.

Daria V. Wright
Friend and Graduate - University of Mexico

INTRODUCTION

Hello to all! Thank you for deciding to read my book, "Questions We All Have Regarding Relationships." This book is designed to offer help those who are either struggling in a relationship or those who have questions regarding the changing culture in contemporary dating. I believe you will find that the questions and answers covered in this book to be beneficial because at some point in our lives we all have gone through, are going through, or will go through trying times in our romantic relationships. I hope you will find this book to be a valuable resource or guide to help you discover solutions to your own relationship problems or dilemmas.

I was eager to complete this book to help others experiencing difficult circumstances in their relationships after my sister, Fertamia Smith, was murdered by the insecure father of her children. Soon after my sister's passing, I started a blog and launched an informal, non-scientific survey on a very expansive social networking site. I posted various questions regarding relationships and readers responded. Inspired by their answers, I was motivated to write this book to document our discussion. While I do not consider myself a relationship guru, or claim to be a "Dr. Phil", I do believe God put it on my heart to write this book to help people by providing insights into contemporary adult relationships. Some of the challenges I faced in my own relationships are included in this book, but in the interest of privacy no individuals are specifically identified. These personal struggles are included only to help those facing similar challenges. It took five long months of writing, re-writing, and more writing to complete this book. I persevered and feel good about the final result. Even though this is a small, condensed handbook, I hope it proves helpful and insightful for all who purchase it. I also hope that through it, someone might receive encouragement for dealing with troubling issues in their relationships and find courage to extricate him or herself from an abusive relationship if they find themselves in one.

Thanks for all of your support!

Kyle Smith
The Author

TABLE OF CONTENTS

CHAPTER 1- Most Important Traits of a Relationship 11
CHAPTER 2- Money and the First Date 23
CHAPTER 3- Relationships with Children 31
CHAPTER 4- Parents Getting Involved 41
CHAPTER 5- Dealing with Cheaters 51
CHAPTER 6- A Dominating Mate 61
CHAPTER 7- Dating Your Best Friend 71
CHAPTER 8- When to Talk to Others 81
CHAPTER 9- Personality Changes 89
CHAPTER 10- One-sided Romances 97
CHAPTER 11- When to Break or End Everything 105
CHAPTER 12- The Physical Relationship 113
CHAPTER 13- Add in the SPICE! 121
CHAPTER 14- Getting over the Past 129
CHAPTER 15- Putting Them First 137
CHAPTER 16- FINAL THOUGHTS 143

CHAPTER 1-

Most Important Traits of a Relationship

QUESTION:

What are the most important traits of a good relationship?

When I first met one young lady, I completely fell in love with her physical appearance. She had everything a man could ever dream of— the perfect smile, the perfect waist, and a nice face! Even though I could not go a day without gazing into her eyes for at least 40 seconds of every minute, she did not even seem to notice my obvious affection for her. As time went on, I began to discern differences in her emotions and expressions. The more I observed, the more I began see beyond the external façade and understand who she truly was. There were times we would not talk to each other because of her attitude. She would always want her way and get mad when she did not get it. She would use her physical appearance as a demand for respect and make comments like, "with my looks, I can have any man I want." Her behavior became so obnoxious; it actually prompted me to back out of the relationship early. After dealing with her negativity, I began to realize I had spent almost a year wasting my time. Her attitude and character certainly did not match her looks. What's more, she was not making a positive contribution to our relationship. I learned from that experience that external beauty is not enough and that good relationships are characterized by three very important traits: communication, trust, and true love.

    Communication is obviously a key factor in any relationship. When a problem arises in your relationship, it is never good to ignore your mate. This just creates more problems. I can not stand to see a couple sitting together at a gathering not saying a word to each other, yet they laugh and joke with everyone else. This is so annoying to me. I remember the times I would ride in the car with my ex-girl friend. When a small argument started between us, she would intentionally stare out the window even as I tried to get an understanding of what had upset her. Just because someone gets upset, it does not mean he or she should be silent and

Questions We All Have Regarding Relationships

shutdown communication. I truly believe a lack of communication builds up tension and strife internally and eventually leads to an external outburst.

When I embarked on my research for this book, I posted several relationship questions regarding communication in my survey. It seems that the decision to stop communicating totally depends on the nature and extent of the conflict at hand. Sometimes it is ok to let your mate catch a breather after an argument, but never for too long.

We are living in a time with multiple distractions which can potentially interfere with our relationships. The internet, phone calls, work, friends, etc are all distractions which can threaten communication with our mates. Whatever happened to the time when couples would fuss and fight and later attempt to work it out? In this generation, it seems as soon as an argument begins, somebody is ready to walk right out the door. The unwillingness to communicate does not solve the problem, it actually makes it worse. Talking things out with your mate not only strengthens the relationship, it also helps both parties get to know and understand one another better. The stronger the bitterness arising from a lack of communication, the easier it is to choose a way out. There is always someone out there willing to take over where the other person has left off. Therefore, effective communication is crucial if a relationship is to survive. One can not expect someone else to understand his or her concerns if he or she never speaks up. Since no one really has mind reading capabilities, a couple must commit to communicate in order to make their relationship work.

If some relationships suffer from a lack of communication, others are beset with the problem of miscommunication or sending unclear messages. Some examples of miscommunication include hearing the wrong thing, blaming someone without obtaining a full explanation, jumping the gun, or using insufficient evidence to arrive at a conclusion. Unfortunately, miscommunication occurs in almost every relationship. Imagine what could happen if a pilot did not communicate clearly with the control tower? Any number of things could go terribly wrong. The pilot could easily end up in the wrong location, or be ignorant of the proximity of other airplanes or the ground conditions which could lead to an unintended or disastrous outcome. This analogy can be applied to relationships because the same sort of thing can happen when there is miscommunication.

Questions We All Have Regarding Relationships

Sending unclear messages is sure to create undesirable outcomes when neither the male nor female really understand the other's perspective. In the long run, this would not only affect them but their children who might eventually feel neglected and begin treating each other the same way.

To take it one step further, couples also need to know not only what to say but the right time to voice concerns. I can remember times when my girlfriend would say something to me to me and I would be so upset that the only thing that came out of my mouth was yelling and foul language. Then when the tables were turned and she did the same to me, I did not like it at all. We must always remember that in relationships, we are two different individuals and we come into a relationship with totally different backgrounds, personalities, traits, morals, values, etc. The only way to get to know the other sides of your partner is through good COMMUNICATION! When there is effective communication there is a greater likelihood that you will gain trust in your mate, which leads me to the next trait in strong relationships.

TRUST is an essential trait of every good relationship. If you are not going to be honest with your mate and they can not trust you completely, there really is no need to even bother with a relationship. It is very hard to trust someone that lies all the time because lying has a snowball effect since one lie tends to lead to another. Sometimes people lie just because it makes them feel better, but habitual lying is often damaging in a relationship. When someone loves another with all their heart and that person lies to them, it erodes the trust between them.

Once that trust is gone, two things arise: accusations and questioning. Usually, it is harder to gain a woman's trust back then it is a man. When a man lies to a woman and does something he said he would not, the woman starts being very careful about letting the same thing happen twice so she observes his every move. Once she completely loses trust in him, the relationship is pretty much over because it is difficult to regain trust. That is why it is good to just be honest and not hold back. I have realized that when people lie to each other, they do it out of fear, because they believe that lying will make matters better since they hope the issue will stay in the dark forever. Most often, the mate will eventually find out the truth. Meanwhile, the lie makes matters worse. If only the truth had been told in the beginning, one could avoid

Questions We All Have Regarding Relationships

much heartache! This goes right back to the need for proper communication for its absence can destroy a relationship.

Here's a good example. A friend of mine had a lady friend that he had known for a long time but his girlfriend knew nothing about this woman. As it turns out, this lady friend was in the early stages of pregnancy. I warned my friend to tell his girlfriend about the pregnancy to prevent any controversy in his current relationship but he did not follow my advice. He withheld the information from his girlfriend and it proved detrimental to their relationship. After his former lady friend had the baby, his girlfriend found out from a message left it on his voicemail. After that discovery, the girlfriend had a complete temper tantrum and ended up hitting him in the face multiple times and kicking him out the house. Now, if he would have told her from the beginning about the pregnancy, maybe his girlfriend might have reacted differently.

The above example, illustrates why trust and communication go hand in hand! In order for your mate to have trust, there must be a level of communication and honesty. We must practice effective communication and honesty on a continual basis. Once we master these two qualities in a relationship, you are ready to experience the third most important trait, LOVE!

LOVE is more than just a four-letter word. It requires a strong commitment and unselfish behavior. Jesus teaches us to love the Lord God with all our heart and to love our neighbor as ourselves (Mark 12:30-31). God is love and He commands us to love. It is possible albeit difficult at times but in the Old Testament, we are warned that "Hatred stirs up dissension, but love covers all wrong" (Proverbs 10:12). To love others carries a huge responsibility.

When I was growing up, I remember how some men used to be scared to use the word love. They knew that if they told a woman "I love you," it would stir up some uncontrollable emotions. I believe a part of them understood that love is not just a word, but also an action. It really means little to say I love you, unless your words are matched with action. I have seen many men leave their women after she gained weight, or did not dress like she used to, or because she was too tired to do some household chores. There have also been instances when women left their men because he lost his job, he no longer looked as good as he used to, or he no

Questions We All Have Regarding Relationships

longer made love the way he used to. Frankly, these are not legitimate reasons to leave someone.

Where is the love when you leave someone for such superficial reasons? If you base your relationship on such superficial criteria, you really do not love the other person. You are selfish and eventually it will catch up to you. If you confess you love to someone, you must demonstrate that love by being there for him or her through thick and thin. I watched my mother stay with my dad until he died of a heart attack. Through it all, my mother remained committed to my dad. Now that was a demonstration of true love.

From the very beginning in a relationship, one must discern whether the other person really has love in his or her heart for you. The following are three ways to tell if a person will love you truthfully:

1. Check to see how this person treats his or her family. If someone acts as if they love you, but is rude and disrespectful towards immediate family, watch out! If someone yells and screams at his or her parents or siblings every time a question is asked, you will likely get the same sort of treatment eventually.

2. Determine how this person listens to you in the time of need or emotional distress. If they do not pay attention to you when you are going through the difficult times, where is the love? A person who loves someone else takes the time out to listen and help deal with problems at hand. Someone who does not care or have love for you will want you to listen to their problems but will not return the same courtesy. It is most annoying when you try to explain your problems to your mate, only to discover he or she is not engaged in the conversation.
3. Determine if your mate is truly into you or just out for what you have. Some people know how to put on a good show and act as though they love you until they get what they want. They may just want sex, money, answers to some personal things, or they might just be out to watch your every move. It is always good to pay attention to determine if they are truly committed to you. You will know if someone loves you unconditionally if they show you that they are not after what you have and what you can give them in a relationship.

We must make sure to pay close attention to characteristics and traits that can potentially cause problems in the future before we say, "this is who I'm

Questions We All Have Regarding Relationships

going to spend the rest of my life with". It is sad to say that some people really do come into relationships with ulterior motives. The only way to find out is to test their true motives. Let us look at the following scenario:

SCENARIO: Mike and Tina attempt to resolve an argument in a hurry...

> Tina: Hey Mike, I thought you said you weren't going to talk to Michelle anymore?
>
> Mike: I don't, Tina.
>
> Tina: Well, why is her number on the caller ID?
>
> Mike: Oh yeah, remember. I told you she had asked me if she could "call today for the directions to that job."
>
> Tina: Couldn't she have searched for it on Google?
>
> Mike: Yeah, but I told you she doesn't have internet.
>
> Tina: Oh yeah, you sure did...I forgot. Well, I'm glad you told me...that really could have escalated. Thank you for your honesty honey, I love you.

Kyle Smith

<u>Mike:</u> Anytime sweetie....you know, that's what keeps our relationship growing!

<u>Tina:</u> Yeah, that's true. Next time, I'll ask you without an attitude to prevent an argument.

LESSON LEARNED: Clear communication played a key role in this situation. Mike prevented a serious argument by letting Tina know ahead of time the reason for the phone call.

CHAPTER 2-
Money and the First Date

QUESTION:

Is it wrong for a woman to pay for the first date?

In all honesty, I had to really think hard about the implications before I decided to put this question in my book. In the end, I realized that this question because it is a reflection of the changing times in which we live. Since the success of a relationship may hinge on the first date, it is critical to pay attention carefully! To be sure, that first date can make the difference between a short and a long-term relationship. So let me begin by saying, there are valid arguments for and against a woman paying for the first date.

Kyle Smith

First let's look at my reason for supporting the position that "YES, she should pay." Traditionally men have taken the lead here but times are definitely changing. Whereas in the past men were expected to be the initiator in romance, closing or opening the door for the woman, paying for the food, and paying for the first date, etc., out of respect for a woman, today dating behaviors are changing as women become more financially independent. With women today being so independent as they own businesses, make triple the salary of some men in huge corporations, have equal opportunity rights in the workplace, have the right to vote, and access to work in occupations that were once off-limits to women, one can argue that women can choose to do whatever they like. When it comes to dating, some women feel that when men pay for the date, he expects more than just a dinner and a movie. It seems gone are the days when a man would take a lady out because he liked her and wanted to show her a good time. In this generation, some men act as if the woman is supposed to engage instantly in sexual intercourse with them on the first date! It is due to these changing expectations that some women might offer to split the bill or even pay for the date so not to feel as that they owe

Questions We All Have Regarding Relationships

the man anything. Indeed, it could be considered very generous for a woman to pay for the date on the first night.

Also, if a man does not have the money the first time, it is okay if the woman offers and is kind enough to pay for the date. I am not saying that this is the way it should be always, but if both the man and woman work, and are not married, it should not matter who pays first. Furthermore, if a woman asks a man out on a date, then it should be up to her to pay since she initiated the request. Remember, just because a woman asks a man out on a date does not mean that she is desperate, she might just be impatient waiting on him to make the first move.

I have always felt that we are living in a society where some women expect too much out of a man. I am quite sure that a man would not mind being treated out to a nice dinner and a movie occasionally. Some women do not understand how good it will make a man feel if they were to pay for the first date. That would surely take a burden off his shoulders. If the man could not pay that night this does not make him less of a man, maybe he did not have the money that night and wanted to see a special movie or go to a specific restaurant. However, having the woman always taking the lead could be a sign of her dominating the romance. Instead of the male traditionally paying; her paying first may start a trend and encourage other women to do the same thing.

I remember when my ex-girlfriend bought me some roses for Valentine's Day; it blew my mind away and made my heart melt. The fact that she bought me some roses on our first date out of the kindness of her heart, made me fall head over heels in love with her. That was an amazing moment in the history of my life. It made me realize that a woman does not have to live by the "norm" or "fad" of what every other woman is doing. The fact that I did not even ask or expect her to buy me roses literally brought tears to my eyes. Most people are controlled by society and how people function in society, but being a leader is realizing that one has the right to do whatever he or she wants. A woman should not feel guilty if she decides to do something for a man that other women are not doing, especially if the man has integrity about himself. When my ex-girlfriend bought me roses, she showed me that she was not living by societal expectations; she demonstrated a kind of leadership I admired.

Now for the other side of the argument: "NO, she should not have to pay." Women should not have to pay for

Questions We All Have Regarding Relationships

the first date is because some men out there are just cheap and can not wait for a woman to spend her money on him. The best way to find out if he is cheap is to see if he is going to pull out his wallet before you purchase the tickets at a movie. If he does not even pretend to touch his pocket, that date should be over! Paying for the first date should not even be an option. Do not even give your date the benefit of the doubt, test him and see what type of person he really may be. The best way to find out the type of man you are dating is through conversation. Certain questions over the phone can give one a clear indication of whether or not he cares about using a woman for her finances. If a woman tells a man over the phone that she likes to buy her man everything and take good care of him and he says, "That is what I like too," you can be sure that this man is more interested in that woman's purse than her person. Men have the potential to be gold-diggers also. Users are users no matter what their gender.

    Another reason a woman should not have to pay is because if she shows him that she can pay, he might smell the scent of an "INDEPENDENT" woman. This could be dangerous if she lets him get close to her after the first date. Often, when a man knows that a woman is independent, he

Kyle Smith

will expect more from her than he would if she were not so independent. He notices her great career, house, and investments, and those material things drive him closer to her. That is precisely why details about finances should be kept private until one has the chance to really get to know the other person. If a man is there just to see what he can collect, let that be the last and final date. I favor women paying for the first date only if the man is able to take care of it as well. If he tends to enjoy watching a woman spend her money, he is liable of making a fool out of you. Even though some might say that it is just money, money plays a major role in relationships. Men can sometimes be con artists, so women have to be truly careful. Do not let a man "slick talk" you into doing what you do not want to do. Just pay attention to words and actions and words and this will give you insight about your date. I truly hate to see anyone be mistreated, and in situations like this, women must be careful to make the right decisions.

Men, you have the choice to say yes or no to the woman paying for the first date. Do not try to misuse her, treat her just how you would want to be treated! We all have to understand that whatever we do to others will eventually

Questions We All Have Regarding Relationships

come back on us. If she decides to take care of you that night, make sure you as the man make it even more special so that she will not feel as if she will have to pay for the first date again.

SCENARIO: Dave and Sarah go to the movies for the first time...

<u>Dave:</u> Hey Sarah I did not expect you to show up so early

<u>Sarah:</u> Neither did I...

<u>Dave:</u> Well, let me purchase the tickets before they are sold out.

<u>Sarah:</u> Oh that is nice of you! But you know what, since you offered, I will buy the tickets for the first date.

<u>Dave:</u> Oh wow, are you serious? Well no, I do not think I could let a woman pay for my tickets, especially the FIRST date...that is not right.

<u>Sarah:</u> Do not worry about paying; you are worth me paying for the first time

<u>Dave:</u> Ok...wow thank you beautiful!

Kyle Smith

LESSON LEARNED: Dave's generosity plays a key role. We notice that Dave offered to pay and felt uncomfortable if Sarah paid for the first date. Dave only agreed to allow Sarah to pay for the first date because she made it seem as if it was a special treat that she wanted to give him.

CHAPTER 3-

Relationships with Children

QUESTION:

Is it wise to enter into a relationship with someone who has kids already?

Entering into a relationship with someone that has kids already has its pros and cons. I am definitely not against going into a relationship with someone who has children. However, I feel that I would rather start my own family with someone that has no kids. I once had a friend that went into a relationship with a woman who had three kids and the father was nowhere to be found, or so the woman claimed. My friend was well off financially and he proposed to her. He offered to take care of her and the kids. Now, I was thought that was very generous of him. They got married and two years into the marriage, she claimed she wanted a divorce. My friend could not understand why and neither could I. I could tell he was hurt by her decision. Furthermore, It turns out my friend had not signed a prenuptial agreement—man did that hurt! She divorced him and ended up going back to the father of her children who had been in jail for those two years. She left my friend, took half of his earnings, and did not care how he felt about the divorce. The pain my friend suffered hurt me so deeply. I did not know how to even comfort him in his distress. I told him not to let the divorce get to him because in the end, God has complete control over all things. I mean, when someone is badly hurt in a relationship, what else can you say? Considering the turmoil he was going through, I did not think that my friend would even listen to me. I just told him to be more careful next time and try to figure the motives of an individual before making such a major commitment.

    Truly, there is nothing wrong with dating someone with children if they are up front and let you know what they went through or are currently going through with the child's other biological parent. Looking at the situation from the outside in, it may not always be easy to discern hidden

Questions We All Have Regarding Relationships

agendas. That is why dating or possibly marrying someone with kids can pose such difficulties. One difficulty concerns whether your new date will accept your children for who they are unconditionally. One may wonder if the child has mental or health problem, would this person accept that child and love him or her with tender care? Another concern is whether this new date will allow time for the children to respect him or her as the new parental figure in the house.

Often times, when a new father or mother figure comes around, there could be a level of respect or disrespect depending on the attitude of the child. That does not mean it is right to be disrespectful. It just means one must get to know and understand the child's reasons for being upset. The disrespect the child may display could also have a lot to do with their age. When the child is 10 years old or younger, the potential parent has time to grow and understand that child because he or she is not yet a teenager. On the other hand, when the child is 13 years of age or older, it can be more difficult to earn their respect. When a child is a teenager, it may be hard to give instructions at times. The phrase "You're not my mother or father, so I don't have to listen to you" may become a recurring defense. When kids talk like that to an adult, it could either indicate that he or she truly had a great relationship with the biological parent before they left, or that they have issues with the actions of the adults in the house. In any case, a child really has no right to talk to any adult in a disrespectful tone of voice. When the new mate comes around and the child continues to be disrespectful, it can easily run him or her away. If the motive of the child is to run the new mate away, the parent could miss out on a potentially good person in their life.

Another problem with dating a person with children has to deal with past relationships. To tell the truth, sometimes it is enough to drive a person crazy. I mean, things can be going just fine but the former mate continues to call and be a nuisance, knowing that the call has nothing at all to do with their child. The phrase "misery loves company" is so true when it comes to situations with former partners. If the new mate truly loves the individual, he or she should not let the old mate destroy that new SPICY relationship.

When it comes to relationships, both parties must completely understand each other and come to an agreement. If there are kids, be honest with the other person and let him or her know he or she needs to bond with your kids. There is

Questions We All Have Regarding Relationships

no reason to come into someone's life just for him or her if the love is not equally there for the children. Speaking from experience, I remember the time a man came into my mother's life when I was just five years old. At the beginning, my elder brothers and sisters resisted him because they did not know whether he was a good person; we knew nothing about him. Honestly, I did not know what to think…I was only five. Well, he kept coming around for almost a year before I begin to see that the bond between him, my siblings and me begin to develop. He would buy us all pizza, chips, cookies and everything, which was the life as a kid. However, it took him a little bit of time to grow on all of us and then he became like a father figure. What helped the situation is that my mother would teach us to be respectful to our elders even before her new boyfriend came into the picture. Now raising eleven children with no father figure was not the easiest thing in the world to do…but she did it. The moral of the story is that he never ran out on us. Instead, he began to know us more and more and eventually he became my dad!

Sometimes it just takes longer for the relationship on both sides (the kids and the new person) to develop, but in time things will work out. We must learn to understand the psychological thoughts of people before we rush to judge them. One may act one way for a certain reason, but rather than being quick to run out, give them some time to understand your children. Then after a certain period, you can make your judgments.

I was once asked if it is okay to go back to a person one used to date if that person now has kids with someone else. I do not think going back to a past relationship with someone that had kids by another person is a problem. It really depends on how deep the feelings one has for that person. Sometimes you were not meant to be with someone at a certain time in life. If God allows a second chance, then maybe that is the way it is supposed to go. As I stated earlier, as long as the relationship is not just based on the feelings for the mate, but also on love for the kids, then there is nothing wrong with dating someone from the past who now has children. Remember, just because someone has kids does not make them a bad person. Furthermore, the person with the kids needs to pay close attention to who he or she decides to let come around their kids anyway. This world is full of child molesters, rapist, kidnappers, and murderers. These types of people are out there, and if one is not careful of whom he or

Questions We All Have Regarding Relationships

she decides to let into the lives of their children, they may regret it. Some people come along with this façade of being great, respectful, and outgoing; but, when the parent is not around, their true intention is to rape or kill the child.

In addition, if the dad or mom is a "deadbeat" parent, they should be willing to let someone else come in and fill that void. However, there are some parents out there that have no care in the world about seeing their child until a new person comes along and takes an interest in the child. Then all of a sudden, that "deadbeat" parent wants to jump back on the bandwagon—LET HIM or HER GO! Do not be fooled by the charming voice, or the new gorgeous image that he or she suddenly portrays because deep down on the inside they probably have the same old motives.

I also believe that boundaries should be set before a new person comes into the lives of both the parent and the child. I do not feel that anyone has the right to come into a relationship and act as though they have biological power over a child. They are better off being a positive influence in the child's life first, instead of coming in with a dominating attitude. It is not easy to discipline a child who is not yours; all that does is create strife between the biological parent and the new mate. One should always discipline with words unless the biological parent gives the authority to do otherwise. Be sure to do things with wisdom and integrity. Being a parent is hard, but being a parent to another person's child is even harder. There is nothing wrong with being up front with the potential new mate concerning your child.

Remember, holding back emotions and feelings may lead to a destructive relationship. Be upfront and inform the person about what you want and the rules you have set. Now, if he or she does not understand the need for rules, then kick him or her to the curb with no remorse. Sometimes people hold back their feelings out of fear, but if you would just be bold and upfront about what you expect from your mate, that person will have more respect for you in the end.

SCENARIO: Tyler is at Mary's house for first time, he finally meets her kid...

<u>Mary:</u> Hey Tyler did you want to come back here while I finish this dinner

<u>Tyler:</u> Joseph and I are watching the game and he thinks the Lakers are going to win.

Questions We All Have Regarding Relationships

<u>Mary:</u> Aw, ok.

<u>Joseph:</u> Hey Tyler, my dad never sat and watched a game with me before, thanks!

<u>Tyler:</u> Your welcome young tiger…any time

LESSON LEARNED: A potential mate's acceptance of a child that is not his or her own has to be real and unconditional. If someone comes into your life and claims to love you and not your child, then honestly the love for you is not real. Tyler showed his passion for Joseph by letting him know the care he has for him even though he is not the biological father.

CHAPTER 4-
Parents Getting Involved

QUESTION:

Is it all right when parents get involved in their child's relationships?

It is important that we get to know whom we are dating on our own because a relationship is between the two individuals that are dating or married. Our parents have lived their lives and had their fair share of relationships, and should not be involved in ours. I am not saying that it is wrong for parents to help with the relationship, but they must let their children decide who they feel is right for them. In some countries, parents are the ultimate decision makers when it comes to whom the son or daughter is supposed to marry, but in America, it is quite different culturally. Children have the freedom to marry whomever they want and to decide when they want to marry.

    Some parents are so involved in their children's relationships it is almost as if they are involved in the dating relationship themselves. When a mother has a close relationship with her daughter, I definitely understand her giving insight on how men are or what type of person her daughter should date, but that does not give the mother the right to select the person. For example, sometimes when the parent decides on who looks or acts right for their child, it could be a false judgment. Just because the person may come in with a suit on and have six college degrees, does not mean his intentions are pure. He could be a lawyer, but also could have murdered six people right before he got dressed and came to your house. I know this might sound a little bit "bizarre," but truth is truth. On the other hand, he could be a person with tattoos all over his body who serves God wholeheartedly. It is best to give your child time to get to know the person for himself or herself and not rely on what the potential mate may look like. I know that growing up, many mothers and fathers probably thought I was not a good person for their daughters, but they did not know the potential I had

Questions We All Have Regarding Relationships

and the respect I have for women. Just because a man may wear a fitted cap or a mo-hawk does not make him a bad person, he probably just does not care about what people have to say about his looks. This world is too heavily influenced by physical appearance. It is not the outside that counts; the inside means a lot more.

Now if the child decides to bring the parent into the relationship, it is their decision. I think parents feel that because they are older and been through a lot, they know everything about relationships. Well with time, things change. Things are very different now compared to when our parents were growing up. Women wearing the long skirts and fully covered blouses, and men wearing full suits with ties on a day-to-day basis, are no longer the norm. Wearing baggy pants might not have been acceptable when our parents were growing up, but in this generation, it might be more acceptable. Parents really should not try to control a child's relationship and they should give the child freedom to date or marry whomever he or she pleases.

Actually, when a parent is not around, the child will find a way to do what he or she wants to anyway whether it is right or wrong. The best thing to do is sit and talk to your child about their feelings about their date. Do not try to force your child to be with someone because you as the parent like his or her mate. A perfect example is when my sister ended up having four children with a guy that she was dating. He would always argue with her when the family was not around, but then act like everything was all right when he was around the family. What bothered me was that he was manipulative, jealous, insecure, and did not care about her feelings. My mother would always think he was a good man because he put on a good show in front of her, but behind closed doors, he would yell at my sister and sometimes hit her. When there was a problem in their relationship, he would come to my mother's house and act as if my sister was responsible. The fact that my mother liked him gave him the okay to come around whenever he pleased; but my sister knew who he really was in private.

Years down the line, they eventually split up. Come to find out, he had been a controlling, and abusive individual. My sister decided to move on and get her life back in order with her four kids, but he did not want her to do so. He also did not want her to be with anyone else. He stalked her. She got a restraining order against him and he still came around.

Questions We All Have Regarding Relationships

Through everything, he still projected this outward image that he was really a great person. Because of his image, none of my family ever had a problem with him because his true personality was hidden. Men who are that insecure, jealous, and abusive will keep it a secret until the woman they are pursuing is finally their mate. In my sister's case, her boyfriend was so jealous that he decided that he would put an end to her life (R.I.P. Fertamia Smith). On April 6, 2009, my sister was found dead in the trunk of a car. After that incident, my mother and the rest of my siblings now pay much closer attention to those who come in and out of our lives. As I said, I do not think it is anything wrong with the parents giving insight, but just because a person looks, sounds, and acts innocent in public does not mean they really are innocent.

    Whether or not a parent should be involved in the relationship of their child also depends on the age bracket as well. When children are in elementary school or high school, parents should monitor their child's relationship but not dominate them. For example, a parent can set ground rules like what time to be home or what time to be on and off the phone. Getting your child a personal cell phone is safe only if the parent is monitoring the calls going out and coming in. Otherwise, it is a dangerous device for a child to carry. The "sex-texters" and stalkers in the world today make it necessary for the parent to know who is calling or being called on a child's phone. Now I agree that if the parent does not want the individual over to the house, this is understandable. However, when not around the house, people are people and they are going to do what they feel is right in their eyes. When your child is out of high school and going to college, they are considered adults. Parents should not worry too much about what is going on at college. If they do, they will worry and stress themselves to death. Just pray and make sure that your child is making the correct choices on who he or she decides to date. Children that respect and honor their parents will remember the wise words of a parent when off to college and make wise choices on their own.

Today the government is backing children to an extent that it is hard to discipline the child. One outcome is increasing child pregnancy and lack of respect for parents and elders. When I was growing up, my mother would not use words such as sex, girlfriend, or any other terms referring to relationships, because she knew that would distract me from

Questions We All Have Regarding Relationships

focusing at school. However, in this generation everything a child needs is right on the internet, television, even on the small computers called cellular phones. So if the parent does not bring up sex or relationships, the child will find out one way or another. Just teach the child the rights and wrongs about relationships because hiding it does not help. Often as time progresses, children will hear their friends talk about sex and it will make them curious. You cannot force anyone to do anything they do not want to, but you can give them insight. Ultimately, children must learn to make decisions on their own. If the parents decide on everything a child will do, people they should date, etc., this will hinder the child from making wise decisions. All of a sudden, the child has to "call mommy or daddy" to make decisions he or she should have the common sense to make on their own.

Remember, it is all right to involve your parents with some things in the relationship, but information that you and your mate decide to keep personal should be kept between you and your mate. It is good for parents to learn to limit how involved they get in their child's business.

Kyle Smith

SCENARIO: Sherry asks her mother about a situation in her relationship and her Mom blows it out of proportion...

<u>Sherry</u>: Mom, do you think I should accept Frank's choice to go to the bar with his friends tonight if we had already planned to go to the movies?

<u>Mom</u>: What...What do you mean the bar?

<u>Sherry</u>: Sometimes I feel like I don't give him any time to hang with the guys, so I told him to go ahead.

<u>Mom</u>: You know what, I told you not to marry him. He's selfish and does not care for your feelings.

<u>Sherry</u>: Mom what are you talking about? I just need a yes or a no answer.

<u>Mom</u>: That's it, I'm going to call him right now and tell him he's not going anywhere if you are not with him.

<u>Sherry</u>: What? That's all right. I'll figure it out...you always have to go above and beyond. I knew I should not have asked you...don't worry I'll figure it out.

Questions We All Have Regarding Relationships

<u>Mom:</u> Well, don't ask if you don't want me to tell you the truth.

<u>Sherry:</u> That's not the truth. That's just you being controlling. Good bye mom.

LESSON LEARNED: This situation could have been avoided if the mother would have just given an answer to the question and not all the extra drama. The mother's answer caused the daughter to react indifferently and become angry. The mother did not have to say she would call the husband at all because her daughter was just informing her on what was happening, not asking her to take action.

CHAPTER 5-
Dealing with Cheaters

QUESTION:

Is going back to someone who has cheated on you a wise or unwise decision?

Whether to go back to someone that has cheated on you is a touchy subject for me because I have been there. After someone has cheated on another, to gain that trust back is very difficult. You may try your best to allow him or her back in your heart, but all that comes to mind is how they have cheated. Some have said that when someone cheats it could be for a specific reason—maybe the sex was not great, they may be tired of arguing, or maybe they are not getting enough attention. I do not care what the problem is.

If you are going to cheat, let your mate know and just go be with the person you are going to cheat with in the open. I feel that people that cheat are heartless and do not care about the feelings of their mate. I remember when I found out my girlfriend had cheated on me. I was not expecting to hear it. I treated her like a queen and I spent a lot of time giving her everything. Do not get me wrong, we had our difficulties and things were not always "peachy," but we did have a great relationship. However, for some odd reason she began to accuse me of cheating. I said to her one day, "you know if you continue to accuse me of cheating, I'm going to leave." She continued to accuse me and I left. I left because it was stressful to hear her make accusations with no proof. That was the worst feeling in the world.

So I went to my brother who had gone through the same thing and asked him, "Why is my girl continuously accusing me of cheating?" He said, "Often someone might accuse you of doing certain things because they are doing things that they shouldn't be doing." I told him I did not believe that she was cheating and he asked if I were sure. I

Questions We All Have Regarding Relationships

told him that I was always around her and our love for each other was too strong. He asked if I had ever asked her if she were cheating and I told him that I had never asked. After the discussion with my brother, I decided to go and ask her if she had ever cheated on me. I believed we had the chance to work things out after she had been accusing me, so I approached her in a way that was not rude or obnoxious. I just told her that we needed to talk. I sat down and told her that we both need to be honest with each other to get a clear understanding so that we can grow stronger. I then asked her if she had ever cheated on me. She was quiet, and I knew right then that something was wrong. So I asked if she was going to tell me or not. She admitted, "Yes, I cheated." Immediately, my heart started pounding. My adrenaline was speeding up and I almost began swearing, but I kept my composure. I then asked her with whom and she told me it was the guy she had been hanging with all the time. That crushed me, so I just politely grabbed my jacket and left. I could not work it out because I felt like I was mistreated and accused when she was really the one in the wrong. I never went back and I moved on with my life. I forgave her, but I did not go back. I did not think it was wise to go back because I felt that a person who cheats will do it again if things get a little off track.

Kyle Smith

There really is no valid excuse for cheating. Even the Bible permits divorce is if the spouse commits adultery (Mark 10). Cheating causes physical, emotional, and mental damage. When someone cheats, it not only destroys the relationship, it seriously affects their partner. For one to put so much time and effort into a relationship only to find out that their mate is seeing someone else is devastating and can cause depression. We must learn to love just how we expect to be loved. Many men who cheat on women later want their women to accept them back. However, if a woman cheats on her man, the man is usually not interested in reviving the relationship and will grab his bag and leave. Whether it is the man cheating or the women, I do not think it is right for anyone to cheat. If you feel you have to cheat, just end you current relationship and date the person you are cheating with instead. Another option is to remain single so you do not hurt someone else emotionally.

People just do not understand that "whatever we sow, we will reap." Whatever a person does to someone, it will come back on them. The pain you cause someone else may not return to you right now, but it will come back eventually. There is a show called *Cheaters* on television that actually help

Questions We All Have Regarding Relationships

people investigate whether or not their mate was having an affair with someone else. The videotaped behavior was unbelievable. It revealed just how people who cheat refuse to own up to their infidelity. Often, the cheating spouse or lover would be furious. Even after being discovered, many had the lamest excuses for why they cheated. It was very sad. How could someone say "it's not what it looks like," when he or she is caught in the very act of cheating? That behavior could easily incite a violent response in their mate.

Meanwhile, the host would be subject to threats of violence and swearing. Not to be intimidated, the host remains committed to tracking down cheaters and catching them in the act. The majority of the time, the mate who was cheated on refused to return to the relationship. Now I know some might feel differently about not giving that person a second chance, but it is important to be wise in this sort of situation. The problem is that if you forgive someone who has cheated and you go back to him or her, all that does is create more strife and complications. The individual who has been cheated on might be tempted to exact revenge by also being immoral or they might devise a plan to punish the unfaithful partner. If someone does decide to take that cheater back, he or she should have a very good reason for doing so.

Some men feel as if having two women at once is not cheating —well then, why not tell both women about each other? Cheating is cheating there is no other way to put it. How can someone possibly look their mate in the eye and say, "you know I love you, right," while he is sleeping around with someone else? That is downright heartless and dirty. If the love is truly there in the relationship, then there would not be anyone else involved, it is as simple as that! Ladies, just because a guy knows how to sweet talk you and act like this player who loves you and only you, believe this, he is just a sweet talker, nothing more. I am sure that he is playing every other woman the same way.

To detect if someone is cheating is hard work but what is done in the dark will always come to light. If we are being honest with ourselves, we would admit that there have been plenty of times when we were wondered if we were being cheated on—we searched the phone, checked the pockets, among other things, but we still may not come up with any evidence or proof of cheating. Being overly suspicious just makes us look foolish and crazy. The best thing to do if you

Questions We All Have Regarding Relationships

suspect cheating in your relationship is to pray and ask God to show you the truth. If someone is meant to be in your life, God will make sure of that. If not, God will remove him or her out of your life and put the right person there. We do not have to stay with anyone we do not want to, and the longer we stay with that person, the more our lives will be in total chaos. It all goes back to having trust in someone. We should be able to trust our mate and not expect him or her to go to another person's house when they tell us they are just going to the store.

Finally, you need to strongly consider taking someone back who has cheated because there is a chance they may have been exposed to sexual diseases and infections. There are too many cases of diseases (AIDS, HIV, syphilis, hepatitis, and all sorts of other STDs), today that we need to be careful of. A person who is a cheater puts his partner at risk. When someone decides to cheat and not be tested, his or her partner will have no idea the diseases that person is bringing home. So cheating not only hurts the person who cheated, it can affect the mate and possibly a child if someone gets pregnant.

SCENARIO: Ryan decides to confess to Jackie that he cheated over a year ago…

Ryan: Hey Jackie, I know we are out to dinner and enjoying it, but there is something I must tell you.

Jackie (Smiling): Oh, if you're tired of me not putting the plates up right, then I'm sorry. It's just that I get tired late at night…

Ryan: No, it's not that. I've been having an affair.

Jackie: What? Please tell me I'm being punked. Ashton you better come out here, now.

Ryan: No, it's the truth.

Jackie: Oh my God, I can't believe you're telling me this on our anniversary. You know what? Don't even tell me who it is because that will make me more upset. I'm gonna finish this dinner like a normal person, but when we get home, you had better pack your bags and leave. I don't want to hear another word.

Questions We All Have Regarding Relationships

LESSON LEARNED: The good thing about this situation is that she did not get out of character in public and she handled the situation like a champion. One does not have to stay in a relationship when the other person is keeping secrets. The best thing to do is leave that situation and do not look back.

CHAPTER 6-
A Dominating Mate

QUESTION:

Are women more dominating in relationships today, due to the status, positions, and responsibilities that they hold?

To dominate means to be larger in number, quantity, power, status or importance (www.freedictionay.org). Some women in relationships today might be considered dominating; but, I would say they are dominating in corporate business, not relationships. Neither male nor female should dominate a relationship, they are supposed to work together as a team. Some may believe or think that the woman is taking the role of the man because of her status in society, but everyone is entitled to his or her own opinion. In today's society, the woman is not actually taking the role of a man. Her feeling independent and confident of achieving many of the same goals as a man is not the same as taking the role of a man. She is just living up to her potential, and she may feel like a butterfly coming out of the cocoon.

Traditionally, women were "stay at home wives," caretakers of the kids almost equivalent to a housemaid instead of a wife, while the men would be the one to go out and work. I do not believe relationships were intended for men to be more dominating. Women are supposed to help their mate in the time of need. Now if the man is slacking and not doing his part as a man, then yes, someone has to step in and take authority. However, women are just as strong and smart as men are; they are capable of handling any task or tough situation as well as a man. Men should not expect a woman to be their slave. If they do, it prompts women to despise men and want to be independent and acquire their own possessions.

Relationships are not just for the man to dominate. Both parties have to agree to play an equal role in the relationship. The couple must work as a team in order for the

Questions We All Have Regarding Relationships

relationship to work. If the man would tell the woman to do this or go do that, be this way or that way, that is not a loving relationship. It resembles more of an employer to employee relationship. I truly believe that the man should still be the head of the household because that is how God designed a man's role in the relationship. However, that does not mean he should be controlling and dominating over the household or the woman. Women no longer have to be the subservient partner. They have gone from not being able to serve in the army to becoming the chief ranking officer; from being a housewife to becoming Founders & CEOs of large corporations.

When I was doing the internet survey for this book, one woman shared with me her story of why she was so bitter after her marriage. She met her husband in college and he was a very smart and a persevering individual knowing exactly what he wanted in life. She broke down into segments how her life went from very happy to the point of her having suicidal thoughts. While they were in college she was studying to be a doctor, and he was studying chemical engineering and business. She described him as an individual that never had to ask anybody for anything, if he wanted

Kyle Smith

something he worked hard enough to get it. She said he would tell her things like, "You don't really have to work because I'm going to take care of our family once we are married and I will buy you anything you have ever wanted in life once I graduate." He was telling her that he was going to be successful and she did not have to worry about her degree or becoming successful in her career. He was a few years ahead of her in college, and eventually he graduated and then decided to marry her. She then dropped out of school because she ended up getting pregnant. He started his own business and they were living like superstars, nice gated house, brand new cars and everything. They had three lovely kids together and were going strong for fifteen long successful years. All of a sudden, he was having an affair with a younger woman that the wife found out about and it destroyed their marriage. He got the mistress pregnant and decided to leave his wife with the kids and she had no career to fall back on. In order to become financially stable, she had to totally depend on what he would give her and she never decided to put him on child support or collect alimony. After hearing the woman's bitter story, my heart dropped because she then had to start completely over with her life learning how to survive without her ex-husband in her life. Nevertheless, her story is an

Questions We All Have Regarding Relationships

example of why women need to continue to go after their own careers, and work hard and achieve their own goals. No one on this earth should ever have to depend on someone else to be his or her source of sustenance. He treated her very selfishly and did not have any feelings for her emotions or the kids. This is a world full of greed, power, and deceit. Therefore, women have to learn not to depend on men in a relationship because they can easily be hurt.

Sometimes, situations may cause the relationship to fall into pieces. However, if someone has his or her own success, he or she does not have to worry about depending on that mate for finances. When women earn more income than men do, the relationship should still be equal. I know money means a lot in the relationship, but it is just paper. There should not be a dominating individual in any relationship no matter how much money he or she makes. If the woman brings home all the money and the man cannot find work, he needs to be at home cleaning up and taking care of home. That should not make him feel less of a man. If anything, it proves that he is supportive and caring. Men give your women some time to relax, she should not have to come home and clean up the house right after working 10-12 long hours,

Kyle Smith

it should already be clean. A relationship will remain strong when both parties can work together equally.

In addition, it is not good to boast and brag on the position one holds and how much money one makes, whether it be a man or a woman. What happens when the position and the money are gone? If the love was not real, and was based on what an individual has, then that relationship will soon be over as well. Working together keeps a relationship so much tighter and it shows how real the relationship truly is when things get hectic. The status one holds does not determine who is in control; status has nothing to do with the control in a relationship. Now if I were with someone and she was not making any effort to change or do better for herself, then that is when I would decide to leave. I cannot force someone to want to do better; she has to want to do it on her own.

It is not easy to make an individual change or do better, but if one person is putting forth effort to make the relationship better while the other person has a careless attitude, then just let that person go. One of my closest friends always complained about how tired she is of using all of her finances on the bills and small accessories for the house,

Questions We All Have Regarding Relationships

while her husband spends all of his money on studio equipment, digital gadgets and technological nonsense. Now she makes much more money than he does, but she still feels he needs to step up to the plate and help her out. I suspect it would be frustrating for her to give all her money to cover the bills while he gets to just play around with his money. It sounds like he just cares for himself. I told her to get in some prayer and hear from God. She told me that her situation is one of the reasons why some women become dominating in a relationship when the man is slacking in areas he is supposed to be going half or more than half on.

In order for things to flow smoothly, both parties must work together. If one is working harder than the other is on the relationship, then you can expect the one working harder to become dominating and perhaps anticipate leaving! Let us take a closer look at the following scenario for an example.

SCENARIO: George and Susan debate over who should handle the business affairs…

<u>Susan:</u> George, have you put your money up for the mortgage this month.

<u>George:</u> No, I have to get this piece of equipment for my Panasonic piano to complete my set. I don't understand why I should have to help with that stuff, you make way more than me.

<u>Susan:</u> What do you mean? It doesn't matter how much I make, you need to help me with this stuff. You know what? From now on, if you don't help me with these bills, I'm going to begin to monitor your money and all of it is going to go towards the bills.

<u>George:</u> You know I don't have any money, really.

<u>Susan:</u> Well sell some of your studio equipment. Then we could put that money towards the bills. I'm tired and need help. If you don't want to step up to the plate, you can pack your bags and go…it already feels like I'm working by myself anyway.

LESSON LEARNED: Susan was not dominating. She was just frustrated by the lack of support from her partner. She tried to work things out, but he was not stepping up to the plate. Therefore, she had no other choice but to make a demand for him to use his money on the things that were important around the house. Respecting one another's

Questions We All Have Regarding Relationships

finances plays a major role in the relationship. If one does not respect the other's finances, then that forces the one that makes the most money to dominate the finances. Whereas in times past, the money belonged to both people, nowadays what is yours is yours and what is mine is mine.

CHAPTER 7-
Dating Your Best Friend

QUESTION:

Does dating a long time friend create strife or growth between two individuals?

In my past relationships, I have only dated maybe one or two women I could actually call a "FRIEND." We were so close there was not anything in the world that could tear us apart. I remember we would sit and have long conversations at a restaurant for hours and hours. Laughing, joking, and hanging out was all we did and I loved it! When her family needed anything, I would always be there and vice versa. Everybody, I mean everybody we knew thought we were a couple. People would say things like, "you two look great together," or "when are you going to marry her?" I would laugh at the comments of others, but deep down inside I would think, "Man, she is a beautiful, intelligent and outgoing young lady." Things were great, and I could not go a day without talking to my buddy! I would tell her everything from details about the women I dated all the way to the arguments I had with one of my closest family members; we both just comforted one another. As time progressed, we began to get these strong feelings towards each other. And when I say strong, I mean they were strong. When she would talk about certain guys she liked, I would not like it anymore, and she did not like when I talked about other women. Each of us harbored jealous feelings when hearing about each other's relationships. That is when the question popped up: are we supposed to be together? Man, the room got so quiet one could hear the ants walking. I felt like it was the right time to ask, but in honesty, maybe it was not the right time. Nevertheless, we decided we were going to be a couple and we would let people know that we were together.

Questions We All Have Regarding Relationships

The relationship was cool in the beginning and things were still the same. We still got along well and people still loved when we came around and brought joy to every celebration. Yet, I never knew that she was very jealous. It surprised me and became a huge problem for us. Her jealous ways were so bad; she thought I was dating all the female friends that called my cell phone. Even if a bill collector called me, she would glance over to see whose name popped up on my caller ID. My personality was the exact opposite. I was not a jealous person so if another guy called her phone or maybe one of her female friends, I would simply tell her to tell them I said hello. I feel if there is no trust or understanding in a relationship, there is nothing! So, we dated and it lasted for a while, but the more she continued to tell me I was cheating on her, the more it made me want to leave her. I tried and tried to be patient, but the accusations were driving me insane. Over time, it just did not seem like the relationship was fun for us anymore.

Sometimes, we would see some of the women I have dated in the past in church, and this did not help the jealousy situation at all. She thought I was going back to those women I told her about before we got into a relationship. I just was not feeling her anymore as I did in the beginning. It really hurt me that our friendship was going down the drain. But I was actually seeing who she truly was outside of the friendship, from a relationship perspective. She constantly argued, yelled, and had negative things to say all the time. The constant bickering is not what I expected from someone I considered my friend. To make matters worse, she was the one I thought I was going to marry. As time went on, I told her "I could not do it anymore." Eventually, I left the situation and moved on with my life.

I want to be clear, I am not saying that all friendships turned relationships go bad. I am just saying it hurts worse when the relationship does go bad. The worst feeling ever was losing a good friend over an overrated relationship. I truly believe the relationship could have been better had it not been for the accusations! In a relationship where the couples were once best friends, deciding to take things past friendship can ruin the person individually and the friendship as well. It is unfortunate to see someone I once hung out with everyday, stop speaking to me over a stupid relationship. I am not saying that happens in all relationships, but I know it happens in the majority of them. If someone feels as if he or she is

Questions We All Have Regarding Relationships

going to date their best friend, the best thing to do is get a clear understanding of one another first. One thing we did was let our emotions, thoughts and actions take complete control. I fell in love too quickly and I think if we would have waited and taken our time, we would still be friends.

Sometimes what we think is supposed to be ours, even if we are lusting and dreaming about it, is not meant for us. It is best to pray and go to God for answers in situations when you are confused about what is meant for you. I never thought that in a million years we would completely neglect our friendship. Friends should remain friends no matter what. It is better to date someone who is new in your life and has no idea who you are and what happened in your past. To have that best friend to call on when there is a problem is very beneficial. That best friend is the one to call on when you are going through tough times in a relationship; but if we begin to date that best friend, who else is there to call on? It is very important to consider the hardship of not talking to that best friend anymore if the relationship does not work out.

I also think it is a bad idea for best friends to hook their friends up with someone that is another best friend of yours because this not only divides the friendship, it creates tension between everyone involved if that relationship goes wrong. Imagine hooking your best friend up with someone that might be good to them because you know him or her, but all of a sudden they begin to treat your best friend wrong. His or her bad relationship not only causes drama with you and your best friend, it creates drama for everyone because you become stuck in the middle. There have been some relationships that worked when the couples were best friends first, but not many. I feel that it feels worse to break up with someone that was a close friend, rather than with someone I just met, or someone I dated and not really knew a lot about. It is always good to ask questions and get a complete understanding about the intentions of your friend. How do you know if your friend has an attraction for you and wants to take the relationship further? There are a few indicators.

1. The individual begins to compare himself or herself to someone you complimented. For example, if a young lady walks past and the man says, "she is fine as all outside," and the best friend says "she don't have nothing on me," right away she is informing him that she is also pretty enough for him to date.

Questions We All Have Regarding Relationships

2. When your best friend wants to hang around you 24/7 and not give you time to see any of your other friends and family—beware. This happens because he or she is testing you out to see how much time you may spend with her if you two were together. Eventually "hanging out" will become touchier, there will be less laughing and joking, and more talk about being in a relationship.
3. When someone asks, "Are you two in a relationship…" all of a sudden, he or she may change their answer to "no…not really," indicating uncertainty in their answer. Before there were feelings involved, when asked if you were in a relationship with your best friend she may have answered: "Eww, he is like my brother, I'll never do that." The change in response does give an indication that he or she is possibly interested in dating.
4. Instead of doing something fun, everything begins to be more romantic, including candlelight dinners, buying roses for valentine day, holding hands at the beach, etc. If things begin to get too romantic, the term friendship does not mean anything anymore.

Kyle Smith

The question becomes "when are we going to become a couple?"

Remember it is best to be honest and let the other person know your feelings up front. The worst thing that could happen is letting your friend date someone that will treat him or her bad, when the two of you probably would have been better off together. Whatever happens, do not let the best friend get involved in a relationship that is not healthy. It is okay to jump in and say
"I think we should take a try at dating, before you continue in a bad situation with someone else." If there is no person treating him or her unjustly, then it may be best to remain just friends. In addition, remember no matter whom we decide to let come into our lives, our best friends were there first. Do not begin to treat your best friend wrong in order to make the new mate happy because there is no telling how long that new person will stay around!

Questions We All Have Regarding Relationships

SCENARIO: Jack and Jill have been friends for three years but have now decided they should try dating...

<u>Jack:</u> Hey Jill, I've been doing some thinking. I know we're best friends and have lots of love for one another, maybe we should consider taking it a step further.

<u>Jill:</u> I was thinking the same thing

<u>Jack:</u> Were you? Wow! I didn't know that.

<u>Jill:</u> Well I always wonder what if he gets with someone else and forgets about me. That always pops in my head and that's why I think we should consider being together.

<u>Jack:</u> Well if you're just going to date me because of all the other women that like me, then we would never work out. I think we should just remain friends so that we won't lose what we have as friends.

<u>Jill:</u> Yeah! I think I'm better telling you about the women you date, rather than some other woman telling you about how I am.

(They both start laughing).

LESSON LEARNED: They both decided to remain friends until the time is right. Imagine if they would have started a relationship while she is going through her jealous stage, all hell would have broken loose. It is best to wait on God and hear from HIM; this is when we get the best results!

CHAPTER 8-
When to Talk to Others

QUESTION:

When a couple is having problems, should they take them public with loved ones, or keep them secret?

Before taking the problems in a relationship public, there should always be some time to make sure that both parties agree to do so. There must be an agreement between both parties in the relationship because some people just do not like their business spread to everyone without their consent. More importantly, some things can be talked out and settled between the two individuals before seeking advice from persons that are not involved in the relationship. When problems occur in the relationship, the first thing couples tend to do is call whomever they talk to the most for advice. But why not just try to talk it out with each other! Most often, when couples invite someone else in their business and the person they are telling may have his or her own problems, the advice given may not be viable enough to help the situation. One of the main reasons relationships do not last as long is that people are too quick to pick up the phone, email, text, or even SKYPE, with their best friends about the things that are going on in their relationship. While it is easier to listen to an outsider, it is always a good idea to talk things over with our mates.

One thing I have learned from involving outsiders in my personal relationship is that people hate to hear your problems and then see you go back to the person who caused those problems. The person that you confide in about relationship problems may almost feel as if they have wasted their time listening to you if you turn around and run back to the problem. However, problems will always occur in a relationship, which is all part of getting to know and understand your mate better. One thing to consider is the size of the problem you are facing in the relationship. For instance, when a man is being physically abusive towards a

Questions We All Have Regarding Relationships

woman, this problem should definitely be brought to the attention of a loved one. Letting everyone know the issues that happen in a relationship could begin to make others look at the relationship in a different way. Remember, there are always two sides to every story. When only one person tells his or her version, they can make the other person look bad. One thing that I have chosen to do when someone calls to tell me about what is going on in their relationship is to just listen to what they have to say without input. It is not wise to give feedback to a situation if there is only one side to the story or if not all the details are available.

We all want to "spill the beans" and talk about what is going on in our relationship, but people tend to turn things around and make it look bad intentionally. Involving family or friends in the problem only increases the tension between the family and the mate. Let's say a young lady had a mate whom the mother did not like. If the young lady were to tell the mother about a problem that occurred, all that does is create more tension between the mother and the mate. Some people are really good at perverting and changing a story into what they want it to be but there has to be a level of respect when it comes to disclosing information. If one of the mates has the audacity to tell everybody what is going on in the relationship, the level of communication between the couple must be extremely low. Yet, there is nothing wrong with getting advice from an outside source, if you both are stuck on an issue. If there is an issue that cannot be resolved and both the man and the woman have tried to talk it out to get some understanding, then they should get some outside advice.

    In any case, use wisdom in choosing individuals to confide in because there are some jealous people who may envy your relationship. Envious individuals are those who cannot stand to see others happy. These can be anybody in your life (mother, father, grandmother, cousin, brother, sister, or friends). They watch you in relationship but not with good intentions. While observing how you and your mate complement each other, laugh, joke, etc., they cannot wait to hear something negative about your relationship. The envious person is the one who will try to sabotage the relationships of others. I can remember I was dating this girl for a while and we could talk about everything. I used to notice her friend's jealousy towards our relationship because her and her boyfriend did not have the same type of communication that my girlfriend and I had. The friend's plan was to create strife

Questions We All Have Regarding Relationships

between my ex-girlfriend and me so that we would no longer be together. She would always ask my ex-girlfriend about how our relationship was going to put negative feedback in my ex-girlfriend's ear. I then found out that my ex-girlfriend was telling her everything we talked about and eventually my ex-girlfriend started having belligerent outburst towards me.

It is not hard to know when your mate is talking to someone else about your business; they will start asking questions that they never asked before. Another sign is that your mate will begin to act totally different towards you and let little things begin to bother him or her. There will always be that outsider giving the wrong advice or information just to see the relationship fail. That is why it is not good to involve people in the relationship when problems occur because it starts a lot of false information, which can be exploited to create unnecessary drama.

The worst part is that people really believe they have friends they can trust. Yet remember, that friends can sometimes be more deceiving than someone you would never trust. The exception to the rule would be if someone has a mate that is timid. In this case, one should be able to discuss and communicate with someone outside the relationship because if a secret or problem is held in too long, then it could cause someone to explode in the wrong way towards the wrong individual. We must communicate with one another respectfully more often than we do, in order to avoid unnecessary emotional blowouts. If we choose to show our mate more attention rather than some random person, it will eventually cause the relationship to grow.

SCENARIO: Jan just found a number in Tommy's pocket and has decided to tell her sister (Anne) what happened....

Jan (on the phone): I just can't believe it. Maybe it's an important person's number.

Anne: Girl, now you know the only business that's on that paper is another woman. I told you he wasn't faithful.

Jan: Yeah maybe you are right!

Questions We All Have Regarding Relationships

Tommy: Hey Jan, have you seen my work pants, I have an important piece of paper in them and I really need that.

Jan: Oh yeah, it's right here.

Tommy: Thank you so much, can I have that number, it's very important.

Jan: Well when you call that lady tell her you are my husband, not her's.

Tommy: What? Do you think that's another woman's number?

Jan: I know it is.

Anne (on the phone): He's lying girl!

Tommy: Jan, that is the number for the Vice President of my company. Why would you think that?

Jan: Well Anne said…

Tommy: Oh, Anne…it figures. Well tell Anne to mind her own business and stop trying to destroy ours.

Kyle Smith

LESSONED LEARNED: This relationship could have been destroyed because of a lack of knowledge and trust. Jan should have discussed the issue with her husband first. It is a good thing he took it lightly because the lack of trust and using someone else to talk to other than the mate could have been detrimental.

CHAPTER 9-

Personality Changes

QUESTION:

Why do men and women have a personality change after the start of a relationship?

People do have the tendency to change over time. Just because someone acts a certain way when you first meet them does not mean he or she will act the same once you get to know him or her better. We must understand that as humans our attitudes are temporal, meaning non-eternal or subject to change. A man can look at a woman and think that she is everything he ever wanted, but once he gets to know her, he may find she is like a demon from hell. The same is also true for men. Some people tend to put on a certain façade at the beginning of a relationship and then become this totally different person later on in the relationship. I feel that in a relationship the more both parties are real in the beginning, the stronger the understanding of each other will be as time progresses.

When a man chases after a woman, puts in hard work, and then decides that she is the one he wants to spend the rest of his life with, he wants her to continue to be what she was like when he first pursued her. Who in their right mind wants to be with someone who has hidden agendas and not enough truth? I certainly do not. However, we must understand that there is a word called "deception" and we must be aware of it in romantic relationships. People know how to put on a façade to gain the interest of an individual. Satan is the master of deception, and just as he tricked Eve into eating the forbidden fruit, he tries to deceive us into getting into relationships we know we should not entertain. A woman must also know how to discern when a man is being deceptive. While he is putting in all that hard work to get her to date him, she must not play the game of "cat chasing mouse," but instead she should use her "remote antennas" to read every move he makes. The fact that I am a man, I know that there are certain things we do and ways we act to make a woman believe we like them. But once we have had the dinner

Questions We All Have Regarding Relationships

and eaten all the food on the plate, we are not hungry for the same dish. It seems once we have that woman we have been chasing and she gives her all to us, we seem to lose interest. Then, it is time to go out and look for another one.

Since a woman is a tenderhearted emotional being, she wants to find love in a man that really loves her. That is why women tend to make men chase them and not just give into anyone that asks for their number. As men, we must not play these games with women because it causes them to become emotional and heartbroken. If a woman finally decides to give herself to a man, he should treat her like the queen that she is and always will be. I always abide by the familiar principle to "treat someone like you want to be treated." My female friends would inform me of someone they might be potentially dating whose been chasing them for a while. I make sure to tell them, keep your guards up and do not fall victim to deceit. Make sure you know his motives and intentions before going further.

Women have the tendency to change as well after a man puts his hard work into her for a while. I can remember when I was in love with this one female and she knew she had my heart. I would chase her to the point where I felt like I was demanding her to be in a relationship with me. I was not stalking her, we would just hang together on a daily basis and she would show interest in me in a nonchalant sort of way. She would often hide her signs of liking me, but I would see her interest when other women would come around, and they would laugh at my jokes, or touch me in a nonsexual way. My friend would be staring hard. I would notice her jealousy and act as if I did not but I would tell her about all the women that liked me. I would also tell her I would never give another woman a chance because I wanted her to be "my main squeeze." Eventually, I became upset with my friend because when another female decided to ask me out, I told my friend about it and all of a sudden, she wanted me to be her man. Honestly, though I was a bit upset, I still had interest in her and I agreed to be her man. After we decided to be together, or perhaps I should say after she decided we become a couple, I started to see many other sides of her including insecurity, jealousy, and control. Therefore, I decided to let her know that being a couple was not working for us. After this experience, I made up my mind that the next time I dated, the decision to embark on a relationship would be a mutual one and not one made by the lady alone.

Questions We All Have Regarding Relationships

When considering a relationship, how can you know to determine if the person you are chasing is worthy of your time? Here are three ways to evaluate the situation.

1. Does the person want to be your friend to have conversations with, or do they want you to be in a romantic relationship? Do not let this person know that your motive is to be in a relationship, but do romantic deeds such as buy roses or bring up relationship questions to figure out if he or she is interested in you as a friend or potential mate.
2. Check to see how he or she treats immediate family members, like mother, father, and siblings. I have come to find out that how an individual treats his or her family closely correlates with how he or she will treat their mate over time.
3. Do not wait until the middle of the relationship to find out their goals are for the relationship; ask them at the beginning. Hidden agendas are seriously detrimental to any relationship. Therefore, it is best to ask where he or she plans to be in the next couple of months or years. Do not be afraid to ask someone who is chasing you personal questions. I personally

use the principle: if you want to know something about anything, you have to do the research to find out. A good idea would be to find out more about their family background, which may give a perfect explanation for why a person acts the way they do.

SCENARIO: Mark decides that all of a sudden he does not feel the same way about Karen after four months of dating…

Karen: Mark, we need to talk!

Mark: About what?

Karen: The fact that you've been acting different these last couple of weeks….why is that?

Mark: What are you talking about?

Karen: Well, I feel like you don't like me anymore. I mean, you just don't treat me the same as you used to.

Mark: Honestly, I don't think things are the same anymore. You are not what I expected you to be, and I'm not feeling you that way anymore. But we could still be friends!

<u>Karen:</u> Well, before we go further in this conversation, you chased me, and now that you got me, you not feeling me anymore? I've been through this before and I will not go through this again. You don't have to say anymore, if you're not feeling me anymore, you can move on.

<u>Mark:</u> Why are you acting like this?

<u>Karen:</u> I'm nobody's dummy, you are the one that changed. You basically chased me to have sex, now that you got that, you don't want me anymore. Well I'm through, I'm not going to sit around and wait on you.

LESSON LEARNED: The beautiful thing is that Karen saw the truth in Mark and did not let it go further. If she had stayed, there just would have been more tension between the two of them. Mark on the other hand, was rude for not letting her know ahead of time that his feelings had changed towards her, as a result Karen was left to figure things out alone.

Kyle Smith

If he had told Karen earlier in the relationship, maybe her feelings would not have been so hurt, and they could have mended their friendship at least.

CHAPTER 10-

One-sided Romances

QUESTION:

Is it wrong to maintain friendship with a person that has romantic feelings for you?

If someone is in a relationship and feels that one of their closest friends is "feeling" him or her, it is time to inform that friend "we need to take some time apart." It is natural to like someone because of his or her attractiveness, character, and attitude, but if we cannot control how much someone like us, then we should not be around them if we already in a relationship. What's more, if we are romantically attracted to someone that we hang around on a regular basis, it is not a good thing to continue to do so especially if there is a mate already in the picture. I can never understand why people develop romantic feelings for people who are already in relationships, especially if they know the person. There are more than 6.5 billion people on this earth according to the World's Almanac so why spend so much time and energy trying to pursue someone that is already taken? We have to learn to respect the relationships of others as if it they are our own.

There are a few things that are tolerated in relationships that can only last for so long. Having friends of the opposite sex as a best friend if you are already in a relationship can lead to that friend having intimate knowledge about your relationship, especially if the mate does not know them. Often times, people tend to become attracted to someone based on what they hear about their friend's relationship. If the issues of your relationship are kept between you and your mate, then an outside best friend would not have any basis for an attraction. In the movie "*Brown Sugar*," starring Sanaa Lathan and Tae Diggs there is a scene when the husband was on the phone late at night with his female best friend while his wife was asleep. All of a sudden, she woke up and caught him conversing with his best friend

Questions We All Have Regarding Relationships

and the thing that made her upset was the fact that he barely talked to her and did not show her as much attention as he did the best friend. He would share ideas and secrets with the best friend before it would even get to his wife. To me this behavior is just rude and insane. The Bible says that once a man gets married, his wife becomes first, he shall cleave to her leaving his father and his mother, (Gen 2:24). If someone calls himself or herself a friend of the family, there is no reason for them to have a crush on their friend. If you are a friend with someone that has a mate already, try asking him or her if they have any friends that could be an ideal mate for you. We must understand that any friend that will come between you and your mate is only there to destroy your relationship. If they are not getting the attention they deserve, they will do everything in their power to get what they want from you.

   I can remember when I was dating this young lady for a while who had a real close girl friend. Now at the beginning, I was very cool with the best friend and we all shared good moments together. Yet after some time passed, I would see some of the things she would do to try to make my mate see the bad in me. Every so often, I would warn my mate and let her know how I felt about the situation, but she did not want to listen and thought it was a lie. I would let her know to pay close attention to what her friend would say and do around me, just so she could see that I was not the problem. The worst part is that her friend was attracted to me and tried to hide it, but as adults, we know when someone is truly "feeling us" romantically. Furthermore, she was also going through problems in her own relationship and did not want to see ours do well. In my opinion, she was not a true friend because she was a jealous, egotistical, sadistic human being. A true friend should not ever want to see their friends doing badly. So eventually, my mate would listen to her complain about me, take her advice and we would begin to argue. I would tell her, "If you listen to her over me, then we are not meant to be together." Eventually, we split up and her friend is still with her same boyfriend. That is why it is not good to hang around someone that could potentially be attracted to someone you are dating, because their whole plot will be to destroy your relationship.

A true friend will tell their best friend how they really feel and will do things to help the relationship, not tear it down; unless they feel the two of you should not be together for some other reason. However in my case, I felt that since

Questions We All Have Regarding Relationships

the friend could not be with me, she did not want my girlfriend to have me either. The world is full of people with evil schemes and motives, and in order to figure those people out, we must pray and ask God to give us discernment and understanding. An emotional rollercoaster is real, and if we do not discern those jealous and envious spirits, then we will be taking a long ride on that rollercoaster.

Here is a bit of advice before I end this chapter: advise your friend to be truthful with you and not hold back on anything. The more he or she hangs around you and harbors those feelings, the more that person will eventually become bitter and cause tension between you and your mate. Pay very close attention to the signs that come along from your friends when in you are a relationship. Some friends are not the friends we think they are.

SCENARIO: Terrell invites Erica to a wedding while her boyfriend is out of town…

Terrell: Did you tell Mike you were coming?

Erica: Yeah, he's ok with it.

Terrell: Well, I'm happy he's not here…

Erica: What, why would you say that?

Terrell: Because, I couldn't wait to get some time alone with you, you haven't noticed that?

Erica: What are you talking about? You're acting strange...

Terrell: You know I want you...

Erica: You know what Terrell, I wasn't expecting this. I thought you were Mike's best friend, but I was wrong. Don't call me or invite me to anything else...I just can't believe you.

Terrell: Well I thought you...

Erica: You thought wrong....

LESSON LEARNED: Terrell was being devious by waiting until his friend left out of town to flirt with Erica. Erica was not expecting Terrell's intentions and was just being generous by going to the wedding with him. The next time she will know not to go with Mike's friend if Mike is not with them.

Questions We All Have Regarding Relationships

If she would have decided to tell Mike, there would have been a major problem between him and Terrell. It is best to know your friends motives before introducing them to your mate.

CHAPTER 11-
When to Break or End Everything

QUESTION:

When taking a break from a relationship, is it good to start seeing other people?

Once we get to the point where the relationship comes to a standstill and things are too complicated, then it may be time to take a break from each other. It is not good to spend too much time together if arguments, accusations, or insecurities occur. If you spend more time arguing than loving, this is actually a good time to make the relationship platonic. If the couple decides to take some time apart, there is no reason that there should be physical contact between them because it may only create more strife. Physical contact may also need to be limited depending on why the couple decides to take a break from one another. Sometimes we as people feel we just need to distance ourselves from each other so that we do not get tired of each other. If one person in the relationship comes off as very aggressive and abrupt, it can lead to more arguments when trying to discuss concerns about the relationship. It is always good to approach the issue with a soft low-pitched tone so that argument prevention is the primary goal. We have to learn and understand that speaking soft and gentle is more likely to keep the other person from reacting rudely. Once one person gets the problem out, then communication is open and the root of the problem may be discovered.

    Remember the reason for splitting up with someone who you have been in a relationship with for a while should be valid and a darn good one that the both of you can understand. Feelings play an enormous role when deciding to stop a relationship and it is not easy for anyone to accept it when their mate comes to them and says, "We need some time apart." Resentment may build up immediately. If there is no one else in the picture, this must be communicated clearly in the beginning of the conversation to avoid false

Questions We All Have Regarding Relationships

accusations. Always communicate your true feelings and stipulate that time apart does not constitute a "free pass" to cheat or see other people. It is a chance for both parties to have some time to think about what can be done to better the relationship.

If I were taking a break from my mate, I would never want to take too much time apart from her because that is when thoughts of splitting up for good might come into the picture. Just give each other a couple of days apart and give God that time to speak to you. In the time of praying and hearing from God, He will give you the answer....just try to be patient. If one decides to date another person while apart, do not be afraid to tell your mate about your intentions. Keeping the new relationship a secret may be more hurtful than being up front. We must first discover on our own why we may need time apart from our mates. If the decision to spend time apart is over a small argument, it is pointless and does nothing but increase hostility and invite room for bigger arguments. Small, insignificant disputes should be handled in a lighter more reasonable fashion. Simply put, just try talking it over with one another first. I can vouch from personal experience that the more time a couple spends apart from each other, the closer and closer the couple gets to splitting up for good. It is always good to get advice from a relationship counselor before deciding to take some time off because they can probably help the relationship with positive words.

I have seen so many beautiful relationships go down the drain because one party felt that he or she needed time apart for superficial reasons. Learn to understand one another before just quitting and giving up. The thing that upsets me most is how some people just do not pay any attention to the other person's feelings. There are emotions involved in relationships and people are liable to be deceived by Satan if they are not hearing from God.

If one decides to just take the time apart without informing the other person this is when Satan will try and come in and whisper ungodly advice in one's ear. Satan may say things like: "he or she is cheating; you are not worth anything. Or, you should just end it all, or have a strong drink to forget your problems." If you are not strong emotionally, all these lies will seem like truth. One must be careful and always remember, we are all human, do not let emotions overtake your mind, body, and soul. Your overall well-being is more precious than any man, woman, or material object.

Questions We All Have Regarding Relationships

Remember to put God first and he will give you answers through prayer.

Whatever happens, do not get upset if your mate needs time off. Just make sure to get a logical explanation for why he or she feels they need the time apart. The only time one is free to should date another person is when there is complete closure to the relationship or if both of you decide that outside dating is permissible. Seeing someone else and keeping it a secret from your mate is selfish and akin to cheating. It will only create more tension in the relationship over time.

SCENARIO: Tony and Sarah have decided to take some time apart. Dating other people pops up in their conversation...

<u>Tony:</u> Sarah, I really believe we should talk things over before we discuss dating other people.

<u>Sarah:</u> Tony, we've been through this a million times and I'm tired of it...

<u>Tony:</u> Well, have you been seeing someone else?

Sarah: Well, not quite...but we have been talking on the phone.

Tony: Are you serious? I've been faithful to you and really trusted that you would do the same.

Sarah: Tony, we have been going through the same thing over and over again...I think it's time we see other people.

Tony: Well, that's what you should have said at first instead of doing it behind my back...now I don't know what to do or how to trust you anymore.

Sarah: It's not like that Tony, I would have told you, but you would have gotten mad...I'm sorry!

Tony: Wow...I can't believe this, I've been faithful, and you're talking to someone else. You know what, this time I'm done and I don't want to have anything else to do with you

Sarah: But Tony, we...

Tony: I'm done...I'll get my things in the morning.

Questions We All Have Regarding Relationships

LESSON LEARNED: In this scenario there are a few key points to pay attention to:

1. If Sarah would have told him that she was considering seeing someone else from the beginning, it could have prevented the complete breakdown of the relationship.
2. Both parties must be precise on what constitutes dating other people to make things clear. They should agree whether they are ready to see other people.
3. Be careful not to move into another relationship too quickly, especially if there has not been complete closure in your former relationship.

CHAPTER 12-
The Physical Relationship

QUESTION:

What should you do if your mate withholds sex from you?

Sex is symbolic of unity and it can either keep a relationship spicy or cause division. If one decides to withhold sex in a relationship for no reason, questions and problems will occur. Questions like, "Is there someone else?" "What did I do wrong to you to make you become platonic?" will arise. One must always give an explanation as to why he or she decides to back away from the other sexually before doing so. As human beings, whether male or female, we must understand that sex is part of our nature and is generally expected in intimate relationships. Sex is an action that creates a strong emotional bond between two people which draws them closer together, physically and spiritually. It is wise to investigate the situation, and try to figure out why their mate all of a sudden has decided to become abstinent. Rather than following our instinct to attack the situation aggressively which could lead to a detrimental outcome, use caution. Remember the work of the wise is to think first, and then take actions. Approach your mate with the hope of getting honest answers. We cannot be afraid to ask questions because not doing so may prolong the issue.

It is not a wise decision to approach your mate with a fidgety attitude. Nervousness and fear give the impression that there might already be a problem. Since people are in control of their own body, one must always show respect for their mate. I could honestly say that sex is not the most important part of a relationship, but it is a crucial component. These are just a few tips for both genders when they feel they must withhold sex from their mate:

1. **Men:** Make sure to let her know up front why you want to abstain from sex.

Questions We All Have Regarding Relationships

    a. You are a Christian who does not engage in premarital sex out of obedience to God, or that you are practicing celibacy.
    b. If there is a disease or sickness involved, be forth right, informing her about whatever condition you have. There is no reason for any man to withhold health issues if he is infected with a contagious disease like HIV, AIDS, or syphilis, etc.
    c. Perhaps you just want the relationship to be platonic so that you can get to know her on another level without sex. Let her know if you just want to communicate with her and find out her goals in life before embarking on a physical relationship. Let her know if you want to observe how well she will maintain without sex.
2. **Women:** Do not be afraid to express your feelings concerning why you want to abstain from sex.
    a. Maybe in a previous relationship your boyfriend wanted to have sex all the time and not talk to you afterwards. Now in your new relationship, you want to do things differently.

Let him know if you feel it would be better not to make the new relationship just about sex, but about getting to know each other better as well.
b. You may feel if he gets sex once, he might not come back around. Let him know you are protecting yourself and that you do not want to be hurt emotionally because your feelings for him are stronger than his feeling for you.
c. You are saving yourself for marriage and he is not your potential husband. If he does not have the intentions to marry, let him know that you would rather hold off until you are married.
d. You are not feeling him and lack sexual attraction to him. Let him know that your feelings are romantic but not sexual for him.

When a woman withholds herself sexually from her mate with no explanation it gives him the impression that she is not faithful and she does not want him anymore because someone else is satisfying her needs in that area. That can be dangerous because if he is a faithful man, the abstinence can

Questions We All Have Regarding Relationships

cause him to leave the relationship. The thoughts of a man are different then the thoughts of a woman. If a man feels that his woman is not being honest and faithful, he is quicker to leave the relationship because he can not bear the thought of another man having relations with his woman. Women tend to think differently when a man withholds sex. It causes her to be more negative and insecure causing her to wonder if he still views her the same as he once did.

Women are more influenced by their emotions and feelings than men. A woman always wants to feel desired by and pleasured by her man. She wants to know that she is the only one for him and that she pleases him in every way possible. For example, if a woman comes out in seductive lingerie, sexy perfume, with her face and body looking like she just had a complete makeover, she will be expecting her man's jaws to drop like a cartoon character. Now if his response is an unexcited "that's nice" and continues to watch television, he has completely ruined her moment and her confidence. She now begins to wonder, "What the heck just happened?" His mediocre reaction will squelch her erotic desires and expectations of a great night with her man. If there is no reason for abstaining from sex, he should tell his mate how beautiful she is, turn the television off and welcome the opportunity to give her the moment she deserves. Most men love it when their woman shows them this special attention.

I can remember when I went through this stage in my relationship when my mate decided she would distance herself from me sexually. It irritated me and made me act completely standoffish. I selfishly ignored her wants and needs because she was not fulfilling mine. When she explained why she would not have sex with me, I was reluctant to accept her reason although it was based on personal conviction. She had decided to rededicate her life to Jesus and try to live a sin free life. Looking back, it was hard for me to accept this choice since I was not on the same page as she was spiritually. I was upset that she was refusing to satisfy my desires. As time progressed, her stand challenged me to learn to abstain from sex and rededicate my life to Jesus Christ as well. I truly had to respect her decision and we decided as a couple to wait until marriage. Even though we ended up not getting married, we remained friends because of our relationship with God.

If one decides that sex is not the right thing to do until marriage or that he or she has to completely trust their mate before having sex, withholding sex from each other will be

Questions We All Have Regarding Relationships

more understandable. Remember, communication is the key factor that will help resolve conflicts when discussions about abstinence occur in the relationship!

SCENARIO: Angela decides to abstain from sex, and Danny gets frustrated...

Angela: Danny, please don't touch me that way....

Danny: What, why are you acting like this? It's not like we haven't done it before.

Angela: I just don't want to do that anymore until you put a ring on my finger.

Danny: Are you serious...what's the reason for all of this?

Angela: Well, honestly, I'm trying to live right for the Lord and this is not right.

Danny: Well, I respect that. I don't understand why you just didn't inform me about this from the beginning.

Angela: Well, I was scared you wouldn't talk to me anymore.

Kyle Smith

Danny: You could have been honest, I would've waited.

LESSON LEARNED: The decision to abstain from sex is not the primary issue; the issue is being up front with your mate from the beginning of the relationship. Honesty will help your mate understand your decision and set the proper expectations for the relationship.

CHAPTER 13-
Add in the SPICE!

QUESTION:

What should one do to keep the excitement in the relationship?

How to keep the spice in a relationship is very important because it is easy to fall out of love, but hard to stay in love. The beginning stage of a relationship is exciting as couples engage in communication, touching, and exploring ideas together. For example, after man falls head over heels with in love with a woman, he usually goes all out lavishing attention on her. Over time, his obvious affection seems to diminish as the newness of the relationship gradually fades. Many couples have experienced this pattern. Before you know it, there are experience arguments, fights, and even on and off separations. By learning to regularly add spice to one's relationship, couples can enjoy each other for the long haul. To be sure, keeping that zest and excitement alive takes effort but it is well worth it.

Adding on the spice means thinking creatively of ways to bring variety and romance to your relationship. Just because money is short does not mean a couple has to sit in the house every weekend and watch a movie. Why not try something romantic that is also free like taking your lady to the lakefront for a stroll and just hold her hand? I know when I felt like things were getting kind of boring or shaky in my romantic relationship, I would buy my lady a rose and a card. Never underestimate the effect of buying a simple rose and a card; it can add a surprising boost to your relationship. It is also fun to play games together, like cards, dominos, video games, etc. Choosing a day of the week to sit down and just talk can be a great activity to keep that spice going. Spending a whole day with one another person having long conversations is always a good way to catch up with what is going on in each other's life. It is also a good to share your vision, dreams, and goals for your relationship.

Questions We All Have Regarding Relationships

In your efforts to add spice to your relationship, do not try to mimic what other couples are doing romantically. While there is nothing wrong with asking question or seeking inspiration from other couples, you probably need to tailor your activities to fit your relationship instead of copying exactly what other couples do. We must remember that every relationship is very different and what one couple does for fun might not excite the next couple. For example, a friend of mine and his girlfriend would always play the game *DARE* with *Uno* playing cards. The modified version of the game was fun for them because the person that lost was dared to do whatever was asked of them. The game seemed exciting so I figured I would propose the game to my mate to see whether she would enjoy playing. Her reaction to the game was quite different from my friend's mate because it just was not her "cup of tea." If she had liked the game, then we would have played it more often. But since she did not, I just eliminated it from our activities because a relationship has to represent the mutual feelings of the individuals involved. There has to be respect for the desires of both individuals, and not just the desires of one person. Both people should seek to do things that keep the excitement in the relationship instead of relying on one individual to come up with everything. Maybe one person would like to try to do a caricature of the other person just for fun. Now it might not be the best painting, but the fun and most joyful part of the activity might be watching the mate paint and laughing while being together.

    In the end, relationships are more than just paying bills and going to work. Relationships involve a couple building each other up physically, emotionally, and spiritually. Fun activities always bring out the true character of people. Sitting at home and playing video games all day by oneself is not a good way to involve your mate. Instead, ask her if she wants to play with you. If your mate does not want to do your hobbies then find something that is enjoyable for both of you. Men, do not ignore her as if she were unimportant. Show her some attention because that game will always be there. Women, cleaning the house may not be a fun activity for men, but it is not hard to make it fun. One good way to make it fun is to make it competitive and reward oriented. Try turning mundane tasks into a competition to see who can clean a room better and faster. Then reward the winner. These types of activities relieve stress while providing free recreation for the couple. Age should never be a barrier when it comes to keeping the relationship fun. Both parties can act

Questions We All Have Regarding Relationships

like children with each other if they want. There should be no boundaries to the fun a couple shares. Sharing fun together beats being serious all the time with no time for jokes.

Relationships today struggle to survive because people are so busy and they focus too much on money. Couples used to go places without letting money affect their relationship. Going to an expensive restaurant does not always have to be on the agenda. I can remember when my mate and I would go to McDonalds and spend the little money we had together on a cheeseburger and fries. That was fun because we were together and did not worry about spending $100.00 a plate. The inexpensive happy meals and dollar drinks brought us just as much joy. I remember when we would order our food at fast food restaurants people would look amazed that we were dressed so elegantly. I discovered that those inexpensive outings together could be just as memorable as the expensive ones. So keeping the relationship spicy and fun really does not have to be based on expensive, materialistic gifts or events.

Once, a close friend of mine shared a story about his high school experience. His prom date stood him up with no explanation. Years later, his mate gave him a prom as a gift for his twenty-first birthday, instead of a birthday party. His story brought tears to my eyes and made me realize how beautiful and memorable this expression of love was. Genuine thoughtfulness always adds zest to a relationship.

Without a doubt, creativity and memorable activities are keys to a long lasting relationship! Be alert to signs of boredom in the relationship and inject some new energy. It is unfortunate when one partner makes an effort to spice up the relationship only to discover that some of the things he or she did were inadequate to make their mate feel the joy and spice. Maybe at the time of the event, the other person probably was not in the mood for fun. As we get to know our mates better, we learn their preferences, their attitudes and thought patterns. We discover what keeps them happy or makes them upset. If your partner does not want to do what you want to do at the time, it is not wise to argue and get upset. Instead, be kind and give the person some space. Hopefully, your partner will come around and realize that your intentions were in his or her best interest. If your mate is the type of individual that gets upset about any and everything, then maybe it is time to move on to someone who would appreciate the joyful experiences that you desire to give. In the

Questions We All Have Regarding Relationships

long run, there is no reason to stay in a relationship with someone whose attitude is constantly negative and aggressive. This only causes strife and division. I was taught that whomever you hang around, you will change them or they will change you. I want my mate to acknowledge and accept it when I am showing her a wonderful and joyful time and not make me feel bad because I want to do something exciting and different. Remember, couples should always try to put joy before stress. If they work to flow in that direction first, then the relationship will last longer.

SCENARIO: Tommy comes up with an idea to make Tammy happy and keep the fire burning...

<u>Tammy</u>: Tommy I feel like we need to start doing more things together, I get tired of sitting in the house.

<u>Tommy</u>: Well, don't worry, we'll figure something out.

<u>Tammy</u>: You always say that, we never do anything.

(The doorbell rings)

<u>Tammy</u>: Who is it?

Kyle Smith

(She opens the door, and notices a flower delivery man with a bouquet of flowers)

<u>Tammy:</u> Oh my God, Oh my God! Tommy, are these for me?

<u>Tommy:</u> Yes honey, I've been thinking about us lately and realized we have to spice things up as well. I then ordered you a nice bouquet of flowers, bought you a beautiful red dress, and got us dinner for two at the Chateau Le Café...

<u>Tammy:</u> Thank you so, so, so much sweetie. I love you

<u>Tommy:</u> I love you too!

LESSON LEARNED: Sometimes we do not know what our mate is thinking and how they may feel. Therefore, it may be a good idea to put together random romantic events in order to surprise them. Spontaneous romance is always a great way to spice things up!

CHAPTER 14-

Getting over the Past

QUESTION:

Is it detrimental to put all your time into someone that is not completely over a past relationship?

Getting over a past relationship can be excruciatingly painful. It is not easy to get over someone completely whom we have spent years of our lives with. It is always difficult to suddenly erase those memories associated with that time together. It takes time to get over a long-term relationship and in the process of separation, it is best to get to know who we are as individuals before inviting someone else into our lives. Therefore, be alert to starting relationships on the REBOUND. Usually, this is when someone moves on too fast to the next relationship, taking their old baggage into the new relationship. I compare it to someone who moves into a new place and brings the majority of the old stuff with them. Eventually, that new place will look a lot like the old one.

We must also be careful then to look out for persons coming into our lives who may bring baggage from their previous relationship. If we are not careful, we may allow unnecessary hazards to enter our lives. It is wise to test this new person to see how interested he or she really is in you. Does he or she constantly compare you to their former partner? If he or she continuously mentions their old mate, the individual might be carrying around some emotional baggage. Let that person deal with his or her emotional hang-ups before you welcome them into your life. God made us too valuable and we do not need to subject ourselves to another's insecurities. In the meantime, keep praying and ask God to reveal to you who your mate is really supposed to be.

When someone tells me they are in love with a person who is not completely over their ex-mate, I caution, "If you love yourself, do not put yourself in that disappointing situation." Being in a one-sided relationship is emotionally

Questions We All Have Regarding Relationships

challenging and causes damage to your soul. Sometimes, it can even kill one spiritually. Furthermore, it is a waste of time as you wait for your partner to get over his or her ex. There have been times when a woman would want to date me and I would turn her down because I just would rather stay to myself than subject her to my emotional baggage. I knew I was not over my ex and I did not want them to have to endure my suffering. Instead, I would go about my daily business and not even focus on dating.

Then I discovered during the process of healing that dating can actually help one get over the old relationship more quickly. I ended up dating someone who became very special to me. Eventually my mind and focus went completely towards her. I had to realize that life comes with its trials and tribulations and we must be willing to try new things or else we become the victim of close-minded thinking. In other words, there is nothing wrong with testing the waters, but just remember in testing to be careful.

When one becomes closed- minded and unwilling to move on, it can ultimately cause depression. Do not be afraid to move on and try new things. Put the old relationship behind you because it obviously was not meant to be. For example, if a female dated someone who was abusing her and manipulating her mind, God could send another man to her that is the exact opposite and make her completely forget about the abusive relationship. But, if another person comes along with similar behaviors like her last partner, she should steer clear for there really is no reason to start dating again because abusive relationships are volatile and extremely dangerous.

Just like being in a one-side relationship is a waste of time, so is trying to force someone to forget about their ex. A person will only erase those thoughts of their ex if they truly want to erase them. In order for a relationship to be successful for a new couple, the focus has to be completely on each other and not on the past. As a Christian, God tells us to wait on Him for our mate because in our waiting, God could be preparing someone to be ready to for you. You would not have to worry about who he or she dated, how long ago they broke up, etc., because if this is the right person, God has him or her for YOU and only YOU! Instead of spending time fretting over someone who is still thinking about their ex, that time could be spent praying and believing God for a mate uniquely set apart for you. When God sends that individual,

Questions We All Have Regarding Relationships

you will know because your connection will be magnetic. Conversations will flow smoothly with fewer arguments.

Be truthful with your mate and let him or her know what is really going on in your mind so that he or she can understand just whom they are dealing with. Mention if you have had past relationships, so that if a problem occurs with your ex, it is more easily understood. The growth of a relationship is exponential when both individuals commit to being open and truthful with each other.

SCENARIO: Lesley finds that she's completely attracted to Stanley but notices all the tensions between him and his ex girl-friend.

<u>Stanley:</u> Lesley, I really feel like we are meant to be together.

<u>Lesley:</u> Yeah, I do to, but the situation with you and your ex makes me think differently. I mean, I'm not trying to

fall in love with you while she's still in the picture…I do not want to be anyone's second.

<u>Stanley</u>: It's not like that! We still have some issues we need to deal with and it'll all be over soon.

<u>Lesley</u>: That's what I'm saying…those issues are the problem.

<u>Stanley</u>: It's not like I'm still seeing her, we're just working some things out.

<u>Lesley</u>: What do you mean, "working some things out?" That's what I'm talking about right there. You know what? I'm not going to go any further with this relationship. Until you two are completely separated, I don't think you and me should have anything to do with each other.

<u>Stanley</u>: Lesley, stop this. You and I have been dating for four months and it hasn't been a problem, why is it a problem all of a sudden?

Questions We All Have Regarding Relationships

<u>Lesley:</u> The whole four months we've been dating, she's been getting more attention than I have and I just can't deal with it. Just call me when you are serious about me.

LESSON LEARNED: It is not wise to try to manipulate someone into breaking up with their ex-mate that they are not completely over emotionally. It is best for both parties to let all emotions and feelings clear up before jumping into a new relationship. Once the time is right, things will flow smoothly and if it is meant for the new person to be in your life, it will happen

CHAPTER 15 -

Putting Them First

QUESTION:

Should couples have to make their partners feel eminent in the relationship?

One might ask, what does it mean to be eminent in a relationship? Eminent is an adjective defined as "a person standing above others in ranking, achievements, or importance," (Merriam Webster Thesaurus). No one is that important that he or she should become eminent in a relationship! It is all right to give someone a compliment, acknowledge their achievements or even help them reach their goals, but to put someone in a category of eminence, is almost the same as making them a god. We must be careful how we choose our words and our actions. To put someone on a pedestal of that magnitude is unfair to oneself as well as the person elevated to that level. The love and respect must be equal between two individuals or there is no love at all. Eventually, the person placed on the pedestal will develop a type of arrogance and beguilement which may turn into hatred and distance them from their partner.

    God has given each person an ability to do whatever he or she puts his or her mind to, so no one deserves to be on a pedestal. However, if one partner is lacking ambition, and staggers around in a contentious manner, then that type of attitude will cause unexpected outbursts and issues in the relationship. To make progress, it is best to understand that both parties have the ability to accomplish any goals he or she put effort into.

    If you have more accomplishments in a relationship, for example, there is no reason to disparage your partner. There is no need for self-glorification and self-worship. Avoid putting yourself on a pedestal so high that you make my mate feel less of a human being. Instead, spread the love and encourage your partner. Let him or her know that through hard work and perseverance he or she can also accomplish

Questions We All Have Regarding Relationships

much. Then look for opportunities to congratulate your partner no matter how big or small the accomplishment.

If a relationship becomes too competitive, and one partner is prideful, arrogant, and cocky, the other partner might decide to leave than stay in that tense situation. Too much competeveness in a relationship can eventually wear down a person emotionally and psychologically, and end up pushing the mate further away. The damage that a competitive spirit causes is likely the reason why some mates feel more comfortable talking to people outside of their relationship than discussing certain issues with their partner. No one wants to waste time listening to someone constantly bragging on him or herself, pushing others around, and not recognizing the achievements of others. I certainly do not find it appealing! In fact, it is downright annoying. I have some friends who love to just brag and boast on their achievements. As a result, I rarely answer my phone when they call.

Individuals that put themselves in a place of eminence only do so because of their insecurities. Most of the time, they act cocky or boastful around other people because they do not have many people in their lives to talk to on a regular basis. The truth is if they have no one to entertain their EGO, then they have to subject random people to their self-glorification. Once we learn not to put anyone in a position where they can control us because of their achievements, then they will learn to respect us for who we are and what we already have achieved.

God is a jealous God, and He has blessed us with so much. We need to acknowledge that it is God who gives us the ability to accomplish greatness, not ourselves. Therefore, people have to learn to bring themselves down to a human level and realize that it can all be taken away. Who are we to give ourselves the glory and look at our mate as a non-achieving individual?

We must understand that the person that we are degrading can be the person to help us during our time of greatest hardship and difficulty. Therefore, a certain level of respect for our partners must be there at all times. It is better to uplift your mate, than to down play their strengths. Realizing that the two of you are made to grow with one another emotionally, spiritually, and physically helps the relationship to become stronger and more harmonious!

Questions We All Have Regarding Relationships

SCENARIO: Jodie has to stop putting Elliot on a pedestal; he is becoming too arrogant…

Elliot: Hey sweetie, I got a raise today for $40,000 extra per year…you need to step your game up.

Jodie: That was so rude Elliot, take that back…

Elliot: I was just joking, why are you so sensitive?

Jodie: I'm your woman and all you do is belittle me. Don't forget that I'm the one who was there for you the whole time you were in school when everyone turned their backs on you. All you do is throw your accomplishments in my face and tell me you're joking…I'm sick of it.

Elliot: Wow, I didn't know that's how you felt. You should've informed me of your feelings right when it sounded like I was bragging…

Jodie: I'm your wife, I shouldn't have to inform you about this. That's something you should already know not to do.

Kyle Smith

<u>Elliot:</u> I'm sorry, I will not do that anymore, I really didn't know.

<u>Jodie:</u> Well now you know!

LESSON LEARNED: Some words might not hurt us depending on how they are delivered, but remember the words from someone close to us can hurt the most. In a relationship, it is best to build one another up with confident words and comments. Do not tear each other down because of status or accomplishments. Say words that will inspire and encourage your mate to want to achieve more, instead of words and phrases that will push him or her to want to give up on the relationship!

CHAPTER 16-
FINAL THOUGHTS

Our attempt to create a more perfect relationship will depend on how well we relate to the person we chose as a mate in our lives. One must know who he or she is dating before deciding to call that person your boyfriend or girlfriend/husband or wife. God made every individual different and to really get to know each other takes time and not just love at first sight. A successful relationship involves a lot of communication, respect, trust, and true love. One never truly knows a person until these qualities are developed. If none of these key qualities develops, one can never expect an honest, mature relationship. With that being said, it is always good to ask questions before jumping into a dedicated relationship. One should not assume he or she knows everything about a person because of what was seen or heard from outside sources. Be bold and ask personal questions for your own knowledge before pursuing the relationship.

Nobody wants to be lonely or have a feeling of loneliness while in a relationship. However, it is better to be lonely than to be ignored. Just knowing that your mate will go the extra mile to hear out your problems thoroughly, or pat you on the back and tell you "everything will be all right" when things are in turmoil, is a great source of inspiration. Yet, if someone ignores everything that happens good or bad in his or her mate's personal life, then this is truly loneliness. Everyone should consider himself or herself as a precious jewel. Remember, if someone ignores you, brings only negative vibes, or creates nothing but drama and strife in your life, then allow that person to walk away with no hard feelings. We only live one life and there is no reason to be in a relationship and still be alone. LET THAT INDIVIDUAL GO!

The following quote sums up well the need for people to invest in relationships to make it work:

"Some of the biggest challenges in relationships come from the fact that most people enter a relationship in order to get something: they're trying to find someone

Questions We All Have Regarding Relationships

who's going to make them feel good. In reality, the only way a relationship will last is if you see your relationship as a place that you go to give, and not a place that you go to take." *-Anthony Robbins*

Clearly, going into a relationship with a "how will this benefit me mentality" is the wrong mentality to have. It is not just about YOU, it is about the both of YOU. Get to know a person, and understand their motives before you call the person your potential mate. It is totally up to YOU as to who YOU decide to accommodate in your life. If the right person does not come at a certain time, be patient and wait—in due time, he or she will come.

AUTHOR BIOGRAPHY

Kyle Smith was born and raised in Maywood Illinois, a small city outside of Chicago. He has a passion for writing, and finds time to do so while attending International Academy of Design and Technology majoring in Information Technology. Kyle thrives on inspiring others to live up to their full potential. Born and raised without a consistent father in his life and having only his older brothers and Mother as a father figure, he has managed to overcome adversities and rise to be an outstanding role model in his community. Kyle's favorite bible verse Jeremiah 29:11(NIV) reads: "For I know the plans I have for you," declares the Lord, "plans to prosper you and not to harm you, plans to give you hope and a future."

www.ingramcontent.com/pod-product-compliance
Lightning Source LLC
Chambersburg PA
CBHW020655300426
44112CB00007B/388